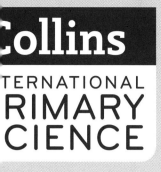

Collins

INTERNATIONAL
PRIMARY
SCIENCE

Progress Book 1

T0321869

Student's Book

William Collins' dream of knowledge for all began with the publication of his first book in 1819.
A self-educated mill worker, he not only enriched millions of lives, but also founded a flourishing publishing house. Today, staying true to this spirit, Collins books are packed with inspiration, innovation and practical expertise. They place you at the centre of a world of possibility and give you exactly what you need to explore it.

Collins. Freedom to teach.

Published by Collins

An imprint of HarperCollins*Publishers*
The News Building, 1 London Bridge Street, London, SE1 9GF, UK

HarperCollins*Publishers*
Macken House, 39/40 Mayor Street Upper, Dublin 1, D01 C9W8, Ireland

Browse the complete Collins catalogue at
www.collins.co.uk

British Library Cataloguing-in-Publication Data
A catalogue record for this publication is available from the British Library.

Author: Tracy Wiles
Publisher: Elaine Higgleton
Product manager: Holly Woolnough
Project manager: Just Content
Copy editor: Karen Williams
Proofreader: Catherine Dakin
Answer checker: Tanya Solomons
Cover designer: Gordon MacGilp
Cover illustration: Ann Paganuzzi
Typesetter: David Jimenez
Illustrator: Ann Paganuzzi
Production controller: Lyndsey Rogers
Printed and bound in Great Britain by Martins the Printers

The publishers gratefully acknowledge the permission granted to reproduce the copyright material in this book. Every effort has been made to trace copyright holders and to obtain their permission for the use of copyright material. The publishers will gladly receive any information enabling them to rectify any error or omission at the first opportunity.

Cambridge International copyright material in this publication is reproduced under licence and remains the intellectual property of Cambridge Assessment International Education

This text has not been through the Cambridge International endorsement process.

Photo acknowledgements
The publishers gratefully acknowledge the permission granted to reproduce the copyright material in this book. Every effort has been made to trace copyright holders and to obtain their permission for the use of copyright material. The publishers will gladly receive any information enabling them to rectify any error or omission at the first opportunity.

P31tl Mj007/Shutterstock; p31tr Altug Galip/Shutterstock; p31bl Mariyana Misaleva/Shutterstock; p31br Angelo Ferraris/Shutterstock; p34t DenisNata/Shutterstock; p34ct Euroshot/Shutterstock; p34c Gualtiero boffi/ Shutterstock; p34cb Gualtiero boffi/Shutterstock; p34b Evgeny Karandaev/Shutterstock; p41t Dragan Milovanovic/ Shutterstock; p41b BlueRingMedia/Shutterstock; p75tl Bon Appetit/Shutterstock; p75tr Roxana Bashyrova/ Shutterstock; p75cl QQQQQQQT/Shutterstock; p75cr Boris Riaposov/Shutterstock; p75bl Lillac/Shutterstock; p75br EpicStockMedia/Shutterstock; p78tl EvaAsh/Shutterstock; p78tr J. Lekavicius/Shutterstock; p78bl Leah Pirone/ Shutterstock; p78br PhilipYb Studio/Shutterstock.

With thanks to the following teachers for reviewing materials in proof and providing valuable feedback: Sylvie Meurein, Nilai International School; Gabriel Kehinde, Avi-Cenna International School; and with thanks to the following teachers who provided feedback during the early development stage: Najihah binti Roslan, Nilai International School.

Contents

Topic 3 Materials

Topic 4 Forces and sound

Topic 5 Electricity and magnetism

Topic 6 Earth and Space

How to use this book

This book is full of questions. Each set of questions can be completed at the end of each unit.

The questions allow you to practise the things you've learned. They will help you understand topics that you might need more practice of. They will also show you the topics that you are most confident with. Your teacher can use your answers to give you feedback and support.

At the end of each test, there is a space to put the date that you completed it. There is also a blank box. Your teacher might use it to:

- sign, when they have marked your answers

- write a short comment on your work.

Date: _____

Now look at and think about each of the *I can* statements.

Pages 7 to 13 include a list of *I can* statements. Once you have finished each set of questions, turn to the *I can* statements. Think about each statement: how easy or hard did you find the topic? For each statement, colour in the face that is closest to how you feel:

☺ I can do this   😐 I'm getting there   ☹ I need some help.

There are three longer Summative Assessments in the book. These can be completed after each block of topics.

I can statements

At the end of each unit, think about each of the *I can* statements and how easy or hard you find the topic. For each statement, colour in the face that is closest to how you feel.

TOPIC 1 Plants			
Unit 1.1 – All about Science	Date:		
I can ask and answer questions to learn about the world.	☺	😐	☹
I can do investigations to help me answer questions.	☺	😐	☹
I can use observations and things that I already know to help make a prediction.	☺	😐	☹
Unit 1.2 – Is it alive?	Date:		
I can say if something is living or non-living.	☺	😐	☹
Unit 1.3 – Plants and animals are living things	Date:		
I can identify plants.	☺	😐	☹
I can identify animals.	☺	😐	☹
I know that plants and animals are living things.	☺	😐	☹
Unit 1.4 – Things that have never been alive	Date:		
I can identify things that were once alive but are now dead.	☺	😐	☹
I can identify things that were never alive.	☺	😐	☹
Unit 1.5 Parts of a plant	Date:		
I can identify and name the roots, stem, flowers and leaves of a plant.	☺	😐	☹
I know that some plants do not have flowers.	☺	😐	☹

I know that some plants have parts we can eat.	😊	😐	☹️
Unit 1.6 What do plants need to survive?	**Date:**		
I know that plants need light and water to grow.	😊	😐	☹️
I know that healthy plants need soil, air and warmth.	😊	😐	☹️
I can say if a plant does not have enough light or water.	😊	😐	☹️
TOPIC 2: Humans and other animals			
Unit 2.1 Parts of the human body	**Date:**		
I can name the different parts of the human body.	😊	😐	☹️
I know that people have the same body parts.	😊	😐	☹️
2.2 Our senses	**Date:**		
I can name the five sense organs.	😊	😐	☹️
I can say what each sense organ is used for.	😊	😐	☹️
I know that we often use more than one sense organ at a time.	😊	😐	☹️
2.3 Using our senses	**Date:**		
I know our senses tell us about our environment.	😊	😐	☹️
I know that our senses help us to keep safe.	😊	😐	☹️
2.4 Users of science	**Date:**		
I know I need to look after my sense organs.	😊	😐	☹️
I know that I need to take care of my eyes and my sight.	😊	😐	☹️
2.5 What do animals need to survive?	**Date:**		
I can list the things humans and other animals need to survive and stay healthy.	😊	😐	☹️

I can say why it is important that we drink clean water.	🙂 😐 🙁

2.6 Humans are similar	Date:
I know that people are called humans.	🙂 😐 🙁
I know that all humans have similar features.	🙂 😐 🙁

2.7 Humans are different	Date:
I know that all humans have different features.	🙂 😐 🙁
I know that humans look different at different ages.	🙂 😐 🙁
I know that some children grow faster than others.	🙂 😐 🙁

TOPIC 3: Materials

3.1 Similar or different?	Date:
I can find features that are the same.	🙂 😐 🙁
I can find features that are different.	🙂 😐 🙁
I can sort things with similar features into groups.	🙂 😐 🙁

3.2 Properties of materials	Date:
I know that different materials have different properties.	🙂 😐 🙁
I know that materials are what objects are made from.	🙂 😐 🙁

3.3 More properties	Date:
I know that materials have many different properties.	🙂 😐 🙁

3.4 What material is it?	Date:
I know there are many different types of materials.	🙂 😐 🙁
I can identify materials found in nature.	🙂 😐 🙁

I can identify materials that are human-made.	😊 😐 ☹️
3.5 More materials	**Date:**
I know that different materials are used to make different objects.	😊 😐 ☹️
I know that the same material can be used to make different objects.	😊 😐 ☹️
I know that some objects are made from more than one type of material.	😊 😐 ☹️
3.6 Sorting materials	**Date:**
I can sort materials into groups.	😊 😐 ☹️
I know that materials in different groups have different properties.	😊 😐 ☹️
3.7 Making smaller groups	**Date:**
I know that there are different types of some materials.	😊 😐 ☹️
I can sort different types of a material into smaller groups based on their properties.	😊 😐 ☹️
3.8 Materials can change shape	**Date:**
I know I can change the shape of some materials by squashing, bending, twisting or stretching them.	😊 😐 ☹️
3.9 Squashing and bending	**Date:**
I know that when I squash something, I am pushing the material together.	😊 😐 ☹️
I know that flexible material can bend easily.	😊 😐 ☹️
I can change the shape of some materials by squashing and bending them.	😊 😐 ☹️
3.10 Stretching and twisting	**Date:**
I know that when I stretch something, I am pulling the material apart.	😊 😐 ☹️
I know that when I twist something, I am stretching and turning it.	😊 😐 ☹️

3.11 Uses of science	Date:		
I know that different materials can be used to make different objects.	🙂	😐	🙁
I know that the properties of materials make them better for some things more than others.	🙂	😐	🙁
TOPIC 4: Forces and sound			
4.1 Thinking and working scientifically	Date:		
I know that instructions tell us how to use equipment.	🙂	😐	🙁
I can record measurements and observations.	🙂	😐	🙁
I can record results in different ways.	🙂	😐	🙁
4.2 Movement	Date:		
I know there are different types of movements.	🙂	😐	🙁
I know that different things can move in different ways.	🙂	😐	🙁
4.3 Pushing and pulling	Date:		
I know there needs to be a force to make an object move.	🙂	😐	🙁
I know there are different types of forces.	🙂	😐	🙁
I know that pushes and pulls are forces.	🙂	😐	🙁
4.4 Pushes and pulls	Date:		
I know I can use forces to do useful jobs.	🙂	😐	🙁
I know water and wind can push with a very big force.	🙂	😐	🙁
4.5 Floating and sinking	Date:		
I know that some objects float.	🙂	😐	🙁
I know that some objects sink.	🙂	😐	🙁

I know that the material and shape of an object can help it to float.	🙂	😐	☹️
4.6 Listen carefully	**Date:**		
I know that sounds are all around me.	🙂	😐	☹️
I know that the source of a sound is where the sound comes from.	🙂	😐	☹️
4.7 What made that sound?	**Date:**		
I know that sounds come from different sources.	🙂	😐	☹️
I know that nature, humans and other animals are all sources of sound.	🙂	😐	☹️
I know that humans can make sounds in different ways.	🙂	😐	☹️
4.8 Loud and quiet sounds	**Date:**		
I know sounds can be loud or quiet.	🙂	😐	☹️
I know that some environments have loud sounds and some have quiet sounds.	🙂	😐	☹️
4.9 Sound and distance	**Date:**		
I know that sound gets quieter the further away I am from the source.	🙂	😐	☹️
TOPIC 5: Electricity and magnetism			
5.1 What things need electricity?	**Date:**		
I know many things need electricity to work.	🙂	😐	☹️
I can identify devices that need mains electricity.	🙂	😐	☹️
I can identify devices that need batteries.	🙂	😐	☹️
5.2 Exploring magnets	**Date:**		
I know that magnetic material will move towards a magnet.	🙂	😐	☹️
I can use magnets to do useful jobs.	🙂	😐	☹️

5.3 History of science	**Date:**
I understand that science is always changing.	🙂 😐 ☹️
I know that life before electricity was very different to life now.	🙂 😐 ☹️
TOPIC 6: Earth and Space	
6.1 Clean water investigation	**Date:**
I can make predictions before doing an investigation.	🙂 😐 ☹️
I can describe what happens during an investigation.	🙂 😐 ☹️
I can do an investigation to find out if my predictions were correct.	🙂 😐 ☹️
6.2 Our planet Earth	**Date:**
I know that Earth is the planet I live on.	🙂 😐 ☹️
I know that most of the Earth's surface is water.	🙂 😐 ☹️
I know that the rest of the Earth's surface is land.	🙂 😐 ☹️
6.3 Science and the environment	**Date:**
I know that water is important for all living things on Earth.	🙂 😐 ☹️
I can help the planet by saving water.	🙂 😐 ☹️
6.4 What is land made of?	**Date:**
I know that land is the Earth's surface that is not covered by water.	🙂 😐 ☹️
I know that land is made of rock and soil.	🙂 😐 ☹️
6.5 The Sun	**Date:**
I know the Sun is a star.	🙂 😐 ☹️
I know the Sun is a source of light and heat.	🙂 😐 ☹️

1 Look at each picture. Then draw a picture to show what will happen next. Why do you think it will happen?

What is happening now?	What will happen next?	Why do you think it will happen?
		_____ _____ _____
		_____ _____ _____
		_____ _____ _____
		_____ _____ _____
		_____ _____ _____

2   There are two flower vases. Vase 1 has water in it. Vase 2 does not have any water.

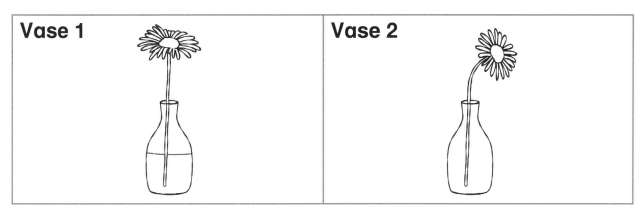

Vase 1	Vase 2

a   What question can you ask to investigate how the flowers will look after five days?

_____

b   What will happen to the flowers after five days? Circle the correct answers.

I think the flower with water will stay the same.   Yes   No

I think the flower with no water will droop.   Yes   No

c   Draw what the two flowers will look like after five days.

Vase 1	Vase 2

d   Do flowers in vases need water to stay alive?

_____

Now look at and think about each of the *I can* statements.

Date: _____

1 Look at the picture. Name the living and the non-living things you can see. Write your answers in the chart.

Living things	Non-living things

2   Find and draw one thing from school that is living. How do you know it is living?

_____

_____

_____

_____

_____

3   Find and draw one thing from school that is non-living. How do you know it is non-living?

_____

_____

_____

_____

_____

_____

_____

Now look at and think about each of the _I can_ statements.

Date: _____

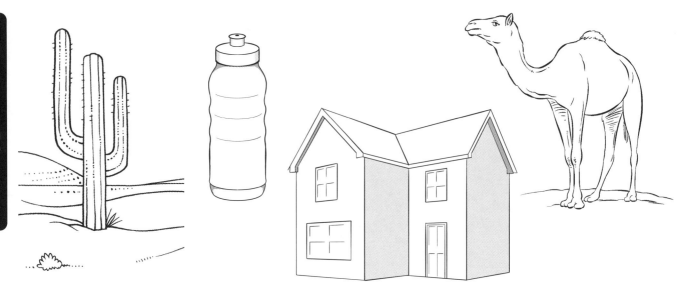

1 Circle the correct answers.

The cactus is a living thing.	Yes	No
The water bottle is a living thing.	Yes	No
The camel is a living thing.	Yes	No
The house is a living thing.	Yes	No

2 Look at the picture. Sort the living things into plants and animals.

frog   duck   flamingo
flower   tortoise
water lily   grass   tree

Plants	Animals

3 Look at the pictures. Answer the questions in the chart.

What living things are they?	_____ _____ _____	_____ _____ _____
How are they the same?	_____ _____ _____	_____ _____ _____
How are they different?	_____ _____ _____	_____ _____ _____

Now look at and think about each of the *I can* statements.

Date: _____

1 Look at the pictures. Tick (✓) if the answer is 'yes'.

	Does it grow?	Does it need food and water to stay alive?	Was it once alive?	Was it never alive?

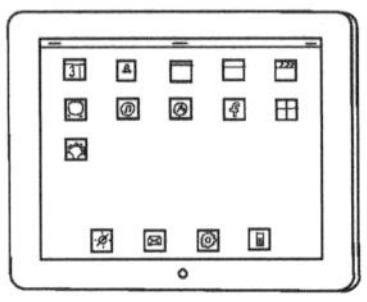				
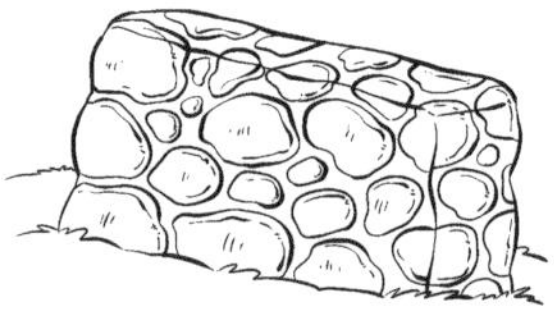				
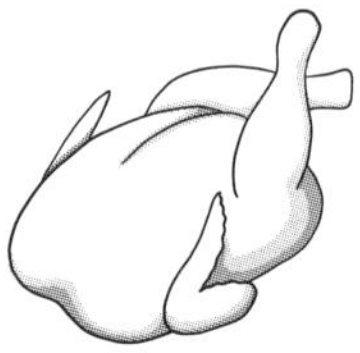				

Draw your own picture.				
Draw your own picture.				

2 Circle the picture that does not belong to each group. Then answer the question.

a

   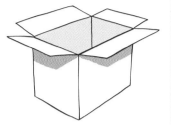

Why does it not belong to the group?

_____

b

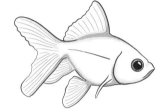   

Why does it not belong to the group?

_____

c

Why does it not belong to the group?

_____

d

Why does it not belong to the group?

_____

Now look at and think about each of the *I can* statements.

Date: _____

1 Draw lines to match the labels to the correct part of the plants.

a

stem

roots

leaf

flower

b

trunk

fruit

roots

leaf

flower

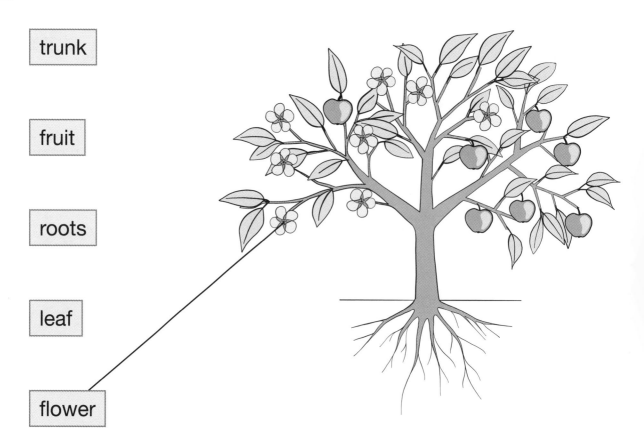

2 Circle the things plants need to grow and stay healthy.

Now look at and think about each of the *I can* statements.

Date: _____

1 Draw lines to match the labels to the correct body part.

head

shoulder

arm

neck

finger

hand

chest

stomach

leg

foot

toe

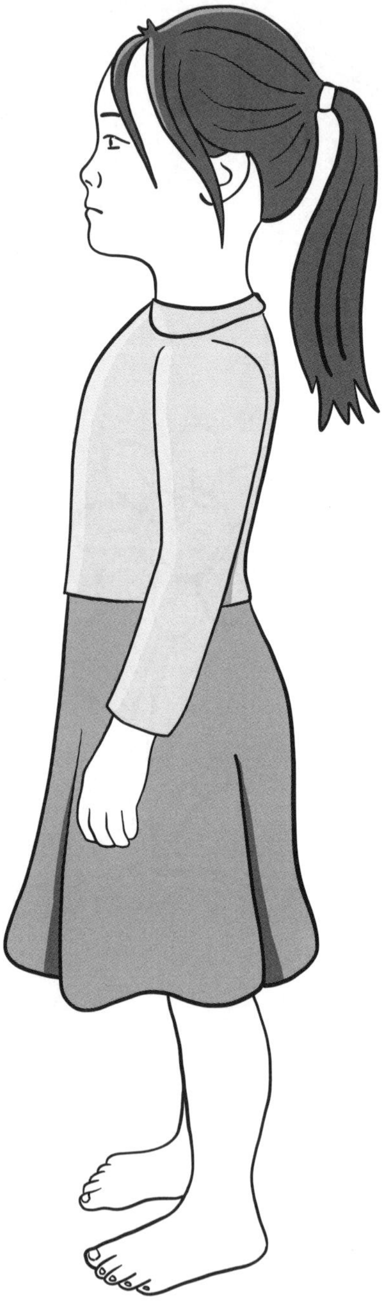

2   How many do you have?

I have _____ hands.

I have _____ legs.

I have _____ fingers.

I have _____ arms.

I have _____ stomach.

I have _____ head.

I have _____ shoulders.

I have _____ neck.

I have _____ feet.

I have _____ toes.

3   On what part of the body do you wear these clothes?
Write your answers.

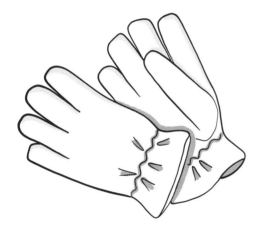

_____

_____

_____

_____

Date: _____

Now look at and think
about each of the
I can statements.

Topic 2 Humans and other animals

1 Choose the correct word from the labels below to complete each sentence.

I see with my _____.

I hear with my _____.

I taste with my _____.

I smell with my _____.

I touch with my _____.

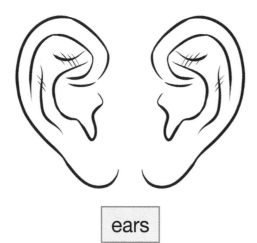

ears

nose

eyes

tongue

hands

2 Which senses do you use to learn more about each picture in the first column? Tick (✓) the sense boxes for each picture.

	👂	👁	👅	👃	✋
fan					
rose					
piano					
writing					
cake					
phone					

Topic 2 Humans and other animals

Now look at and think about each of the *I can* statements.

Date: _____

1 Look at the boy in the picture.

a Circle the correct answer.

Is it safe for the boy to have his eyes closed?   Yes   No

b Give a reason for choosing your answer to part **a**.

I think _____

_____

_____

_____

_____

2 Look at the pictures. Circle the items that help you to keep safe in the dark.

Now look at and think about each of the *I can* statements.

Date: _____

1 What do humans and other animals need to survive?
Write the words in the correct columns.

| air | bricks | ice-cream | toys | food |
| safety | wind | water | warmth | string |

Humans and other animals need …	Humans and other animals do not need …

2 Explain why you would or would not drink the water in each picture.

a

_____

_____

_____

_____

b

_____

_____

_____

c

_____

_____

_____

_____

d

_____

_____

_____

_____

Now look at and think about each of the *I can* statements.

Date: _____

1 Draw lines to match the pictures to the different stages of human life.

baby

toddler

young child

older child

adult

2 Look at the picture of the two children. What features can you see that are similar?

_____

_____

_____

_____

_____

_____

3 Look at the people in the pictures. List all the differences you can see.

Differences between the boys: _____ _____ _____ _____ _____	
Differences between the girl and her mum: _____ _____ _____ _____	
Differences between the two athletes: _____ _____ _____ _____	

Now look at and think about each of the *I can* statements.

Date: _____

1 Look at each picture. Tick (✓) the correct column.

	Alive	Was once alive	Has never been alive
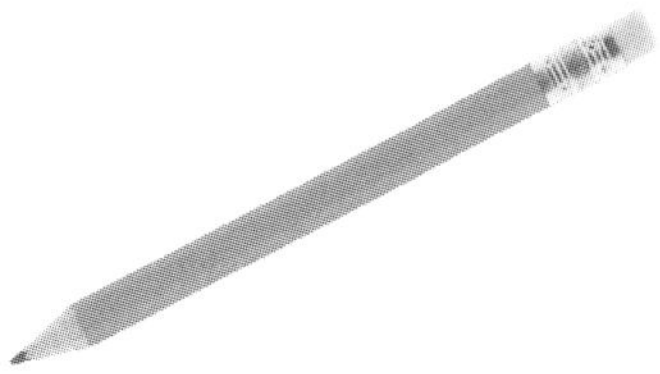			

2 What do the things in question 1 that are alive need to survive?

_____

_____

_____

_____

_____

Plant 1 (living)   **Plant 2 (dead)**

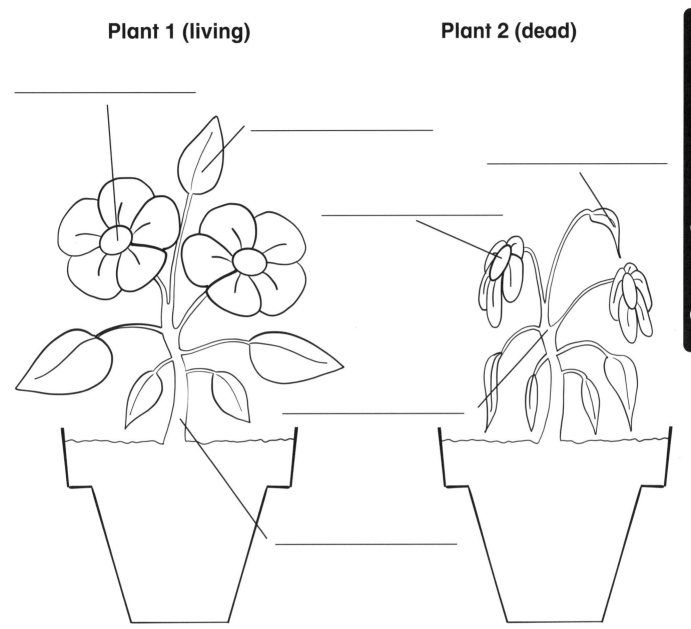

3   Complete the labels on the plants.

4   Draw the important part of the plant that is missing in each drawing.

5   What does Plant 1 need so that it does not start to look like Plant 2?

_____

_____

_____

6 Look at the picture. How is the family using their senses to tell them about the beach?

Sight: _____

_____

_____

_____

Smell: _____

_____

Touch: _____

_____

Hearing: _____

_____

Taste: _____

_____

7 What features can you see that are similar between the humans in the picture?

_____

_____

8 What features can you see that are different between the humans in the picture?

_____

_____

9 Complete the sentences. Use the words in the box. Draw a picture for each sentence.

water   food   air

Sentence	Picture
Animals need _____ to eat.	
Animals need _____ to breathe.	
Animals need _____ to drink.	

Date: _____

1 Circle the picture that does not belong to each group.

a

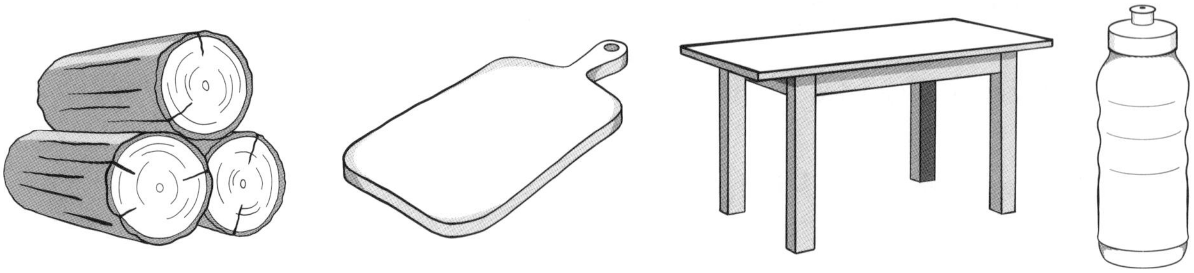

b

c

d

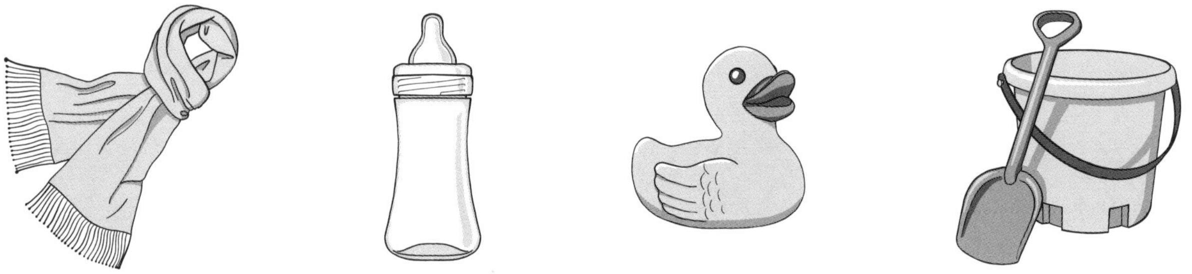

e

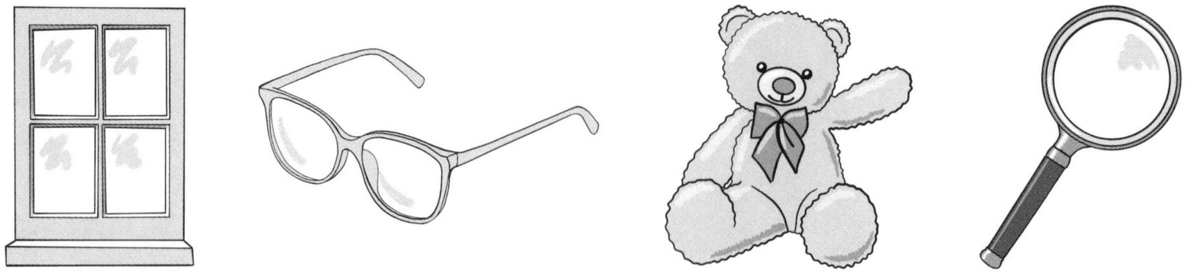

f

2 Write the names of the objects in the correct circles. Some objects may be added to both circles.

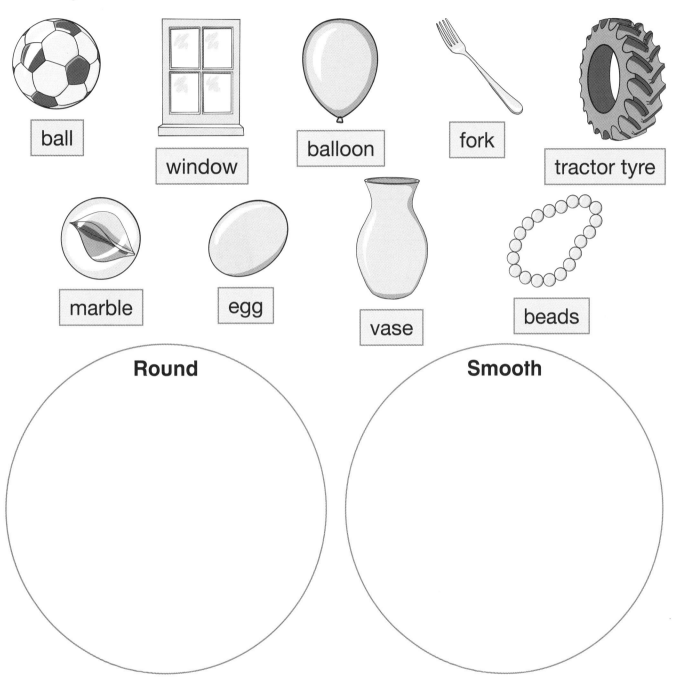

ball

window

balloon

fork

tractor tyre

marble

egg

vase

beads

Round

Smooth

3 Which objects did you add to both circles?

_____

Now look at and think about each of the *I can* statements.

Date: _____

1 Look at the picture. Is the box strong? Why do you think this?

_____

_____

_____

_____

_____

_____

_____

2 Draw a more suitable box for the man to carry his groceries.

3 What properties does the man's box need?

_____

_____

4 Choose the properties that describe each object.

> hard   soft   shiny   dull   smooth   rough
> heavy   light   strong   weak   transparent
> waterproof   flexible   absorbent

Object	Properties
umbrella	
window	
kitchen sponge	
rubber gloves	
aluminium foil	
marbles	

Now look at and think about each of the *I can* statements.

Date: _____

Topic 3 Materials

1 Sort the materials by drawing pictures of them in the correct circles.

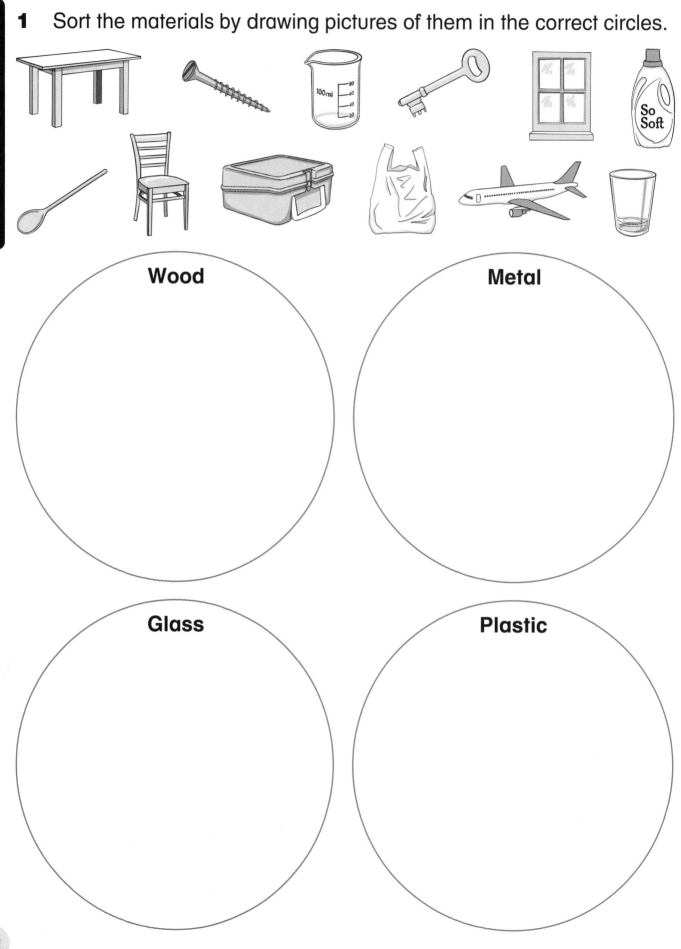

Wood

Metal

Glass

Plastic

2 Which is the odd one out? Explain why.

a paper   cardboard   car

The odd one out is _____

because _____.

b chalk   marbles   glasses

The odd one out is _____

because _____.

c gloves   diamond   wool

The odd one out is _____

because _____.

d book   coins   scissors

The odd one out is _____

because _____.

e aeroplane   newspaper   car

The odd one out is _____

because _____.

Now look at and think about each of the *I can* statements.

Date: _____

1 Tick (✓) the columns that describe the properties of each type of paper.

Paper	strong	weak	thin	thick	smooth	rough	shiny	dull
newspaper								
paper towel								
tissue								
cardboard								
wax paper								
baking paper								
book paper								

2 Draw lines to sort the plastic items into the correct bins. Some items can go in more than one bin.

water bottle

shopping bag

crisp packet

milk bottle

coat hanger

spade

crate

rubbish bag

| Transparent | Very hard | Bends | Thick | Thin |

Now look at and think about each of the *I can* statements.

Date: _____

1 Look at the pictures. How has the shape of the clay been changed? Use the words in the box to help you.

bending   twisting   squashing   stretching

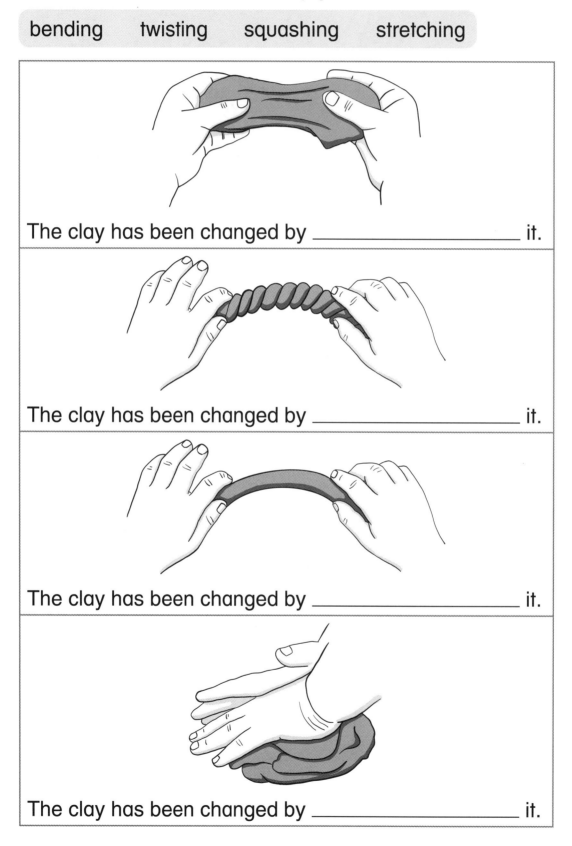

The clay has been changed by _____ it.

The clay has been changed by _____ it.

The clay has been changed by _____ it.

The clay has been changed by _____ it.

2 Tick (✓) the correct boxes to show how the shape of the object can be changed.

Object	Can I stretch it?	Can I bend it?	Can I twist it?	Can I squash it?
elastic band				
water bottle				
sponge				
pipe cleaner				
drinking straw				
woollen hat				
modelling clay				

Topic 3 Materials

Now look at and think about each of the *I can* statements.

Date: _____

Topic 3 Materials

1 Colour in all the objects that you can squash. Tick (✓) the box next to the objects you can bend.

| wooden spoon | ☐ |

| newspaper | ☐ |

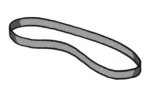

| elastic band | ☐ |

| plastic ruler | ☐ |

| paper | ☐ |

| tomato | ☐ |

| sponge | ☐ |

| ball | ☐ |

| hair comb | ☐ |

2 Tick (✓) the correct sentences.

I can twist a spoon.

I can stretch a balloon.

I can twist a sponge.

I can stretch a clock.

I can twist a T-shirt.

I can stretch a piece of wool.

I can twist a calculator.

I can stretch a torch.

Now look at and think about each of the *I can* statements.

Date: _____

49

1 Look at the pictures. What material is each object made from? What properties does the object have? Write your answers in the chart.

Object	Material	Properties
 drinking glass		
 saucepan		
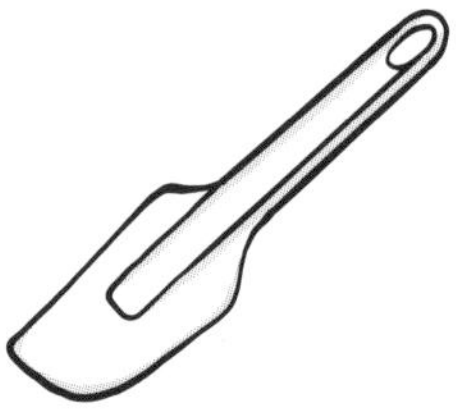 spatula for spreading icing		
 recipe book		
 spoon for stirring hot food on a cooker		

2 Which material is the best for making each object? Choose the word and complete each sentence.

a chair

The best material for a chair is (wood / sponge) because it is _____.

b gloves

The best material for gloves is (wood / wool) because it is

_____.

c candles

The best material for a candle is (metal / wax) because it is

_____.

d storage box

The best material for a storage box is (cardboard / cement) because it is

_____.

e bucket

The best material for a bucket is (plastic / cardboard) because it is

_____.

f fork

The best material for a fork is (sponge / metal) because it is

_____.

Now look at and think about each of the *I can* statements.

Date: _____

1 An investigation is set up to see which toy car travels the furthest when pushed.

a Predict which car will travel the furthest.

_____

b Why do you think this car will travel the furthest?

_____

_____

2 The positions of the cars after they were pushed are shown below.

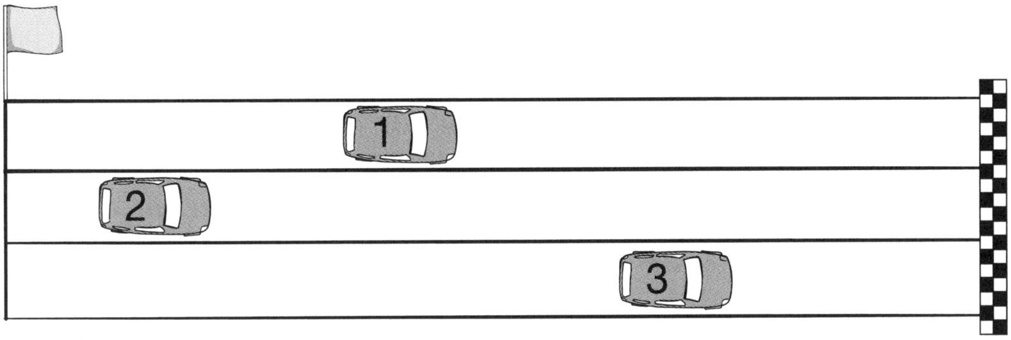

a Use a ruler to measure how far each car travelled from the start to the place where it stopped.

Car	Distance travelled
1	
2	
3	

b What do you think helped the cars to travel further?

_____

3 Look back at your prediction in question **1a**. Were you correct? Tick your answer.

☐ Yes   ☐ No   ☐ Not sure

4 Draw a ramp for a car to travel further than Car 3.

Now look at and think about each of the *I can* statements.

☐

Date: _____

1 Tick (✓) the columns to show how the different animals can move.

Animal	run	fly	crawl	jump	slide	swim
butterfly						
caterpillar						
kangaroo						
fish						
duck						
crocodile						
spider						

a The most common movement among the animals

is _____.

2 Sort the pictures by how the things move or how people move on them. Write them in the correct boxes.

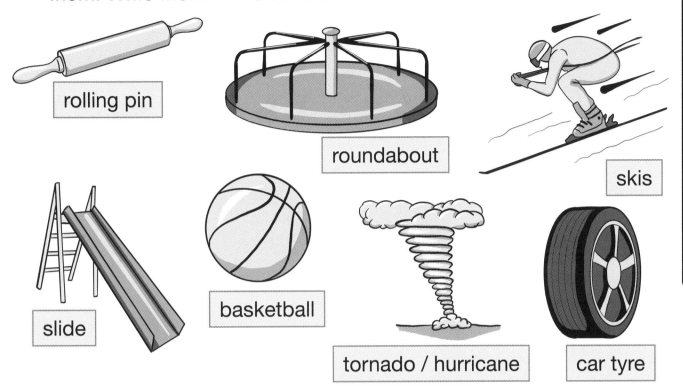

rolling pin

roundabout

skis

slide

basketball

tornado / hurricane

car tyre

Spin	Roll
Slide	**Bounce**

Now look at and think about each of the *I can* statements.

Date: _____

1 Which pictures show a push or a pull? Write **push** or **pull** under each picture.

_____

_____

_____

_____

_____

_____

2 Look at the pictures. Tick (✓) to show whether the wind or water helps to move them.

Object	Wind	Water

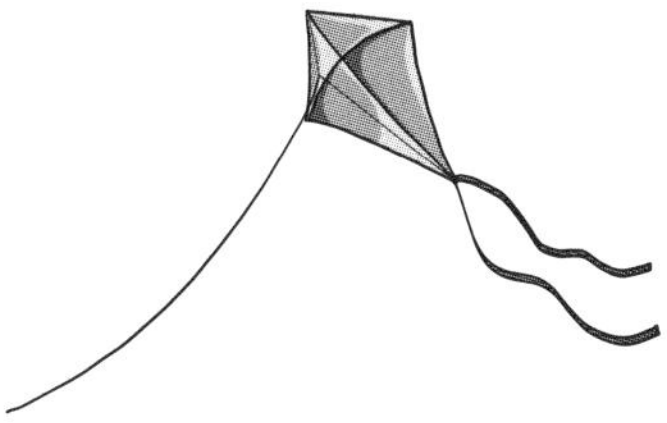		

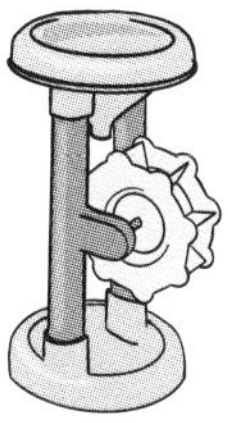		

Now look at and think about each of the *I can* statements.

Date: _____

1 Some objects are put into a bucket of water.

    a Predict whether each object will float or sink.

    b Explain why you think the object will float or sink.

Object	Float or sink?	Why?
 ball		
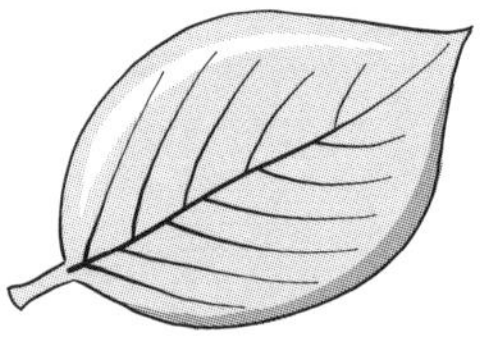 leaf		
 book		
 pine cone		
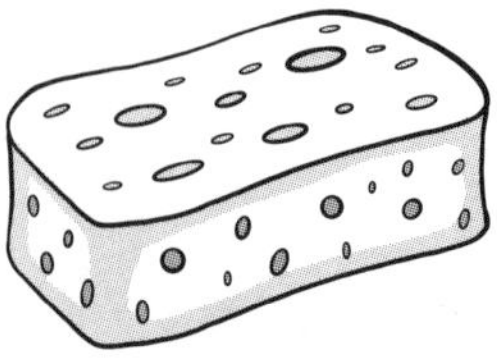 sponge		

2 Look at the picture.

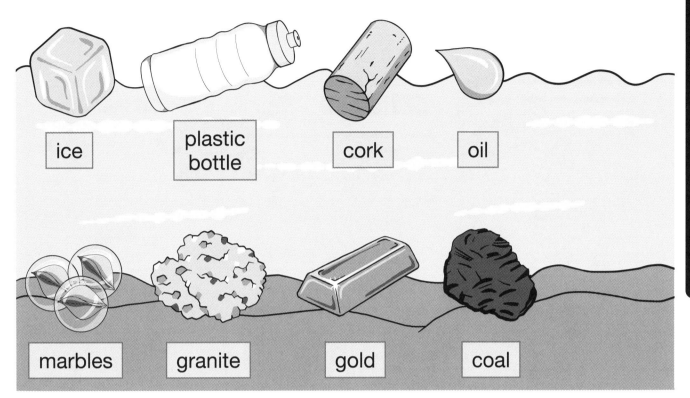

ice | plastic bottle | cork | oil

marbles | granite | gold | coal

a List the objects that float.

_____

b List the objects that sink.

_____

c Draw one more object on the picture that floats.

d What did you draw? Why will it float?

_____

e Draw one more object on the picture that sinks.

f What did you draw? Why will it sink?

_____

Now look at and think about each of the *I can* statements.

Date: _____

Topic 4 Forces and sound

1 Look at the picture.

a Circle the sources of the loud sounds in red.

b Circle the sources of the quiet sounds in blue.

2 Look at the pictures. All the sounds are loud. Decide which sound is the loudest. Order the sounds from the loudest (1) to the least loud (6).

3 Look at the picture. Identify the source of each sound. Use the words in the box.

> leaves of the trees and bushes
>
> dragonflies flying
>
> birds' wings
>
> scorpion and spider walking on the rocks

a What is making the flapping sound?

_____

b What is making the buzzing sound?

_____

c What is making the scuttling noise?

_____

d What is making the rustling noise?

_____

Now look at and think about each of the *I can* statements.

Date: _____

1 Write the different properties of each object.

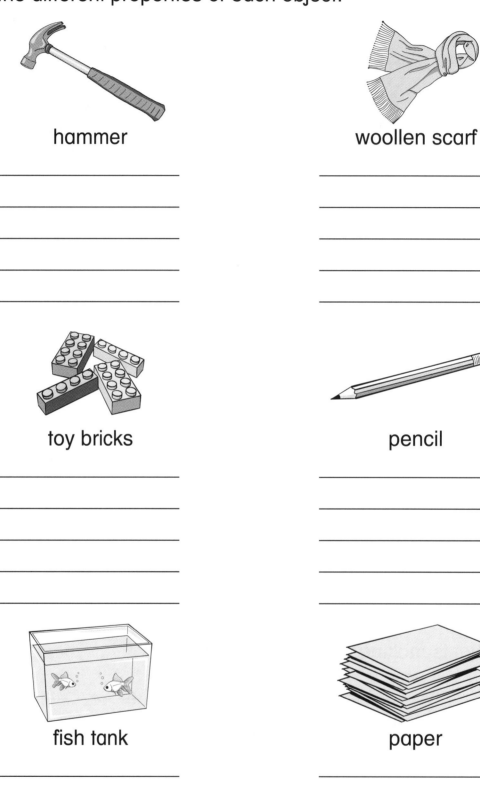

hammer

_____
_____
_____
_____
_____

woollen scarf

_____
_____
_____
_____
_____

toy bricks

_____
_____
_____
_____
_____

pencil

_____
_____
_____
_____
_____

fish tank

_____
_____
_____
_____
_____

paper

_____
_____
_____
_____
_____

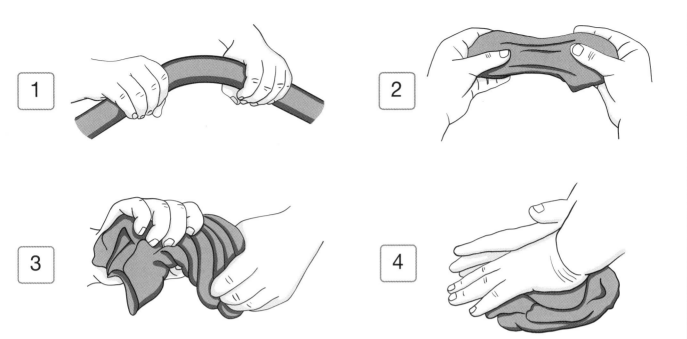

2 What is the person doing to the material in picture 1?

_____

Name another object you can do this to.

_____

3 What is the person doing to the material in picture 2?

_____

Name another material you can do this to.

_____

4 What is the person doing to the material in picture 3?

_____

Name another material you can do this to.

_____

5 What is the person doing to the material in picture 4?

_____

Name another material you can do this to.

_____

6 Look at the picture. What movement will help the children to move?

_____

7 Look at the picture. What movement will help the boy to move forward?

_____

8 Look at the picture. What movement will help the girl to drag the wagon behind her?

_____

9 Avril put the following objects in a glass of water. Predict whether they will sink or float.

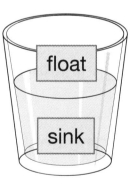

float

sink

 leaf

 coin

 pebble

_____ _____ _____

 key

 drinking straw

 teaspoon

_____ _____ _____

10 Circle all the sources of loud sounds in the picture. Draw two objects that make quiet sounds in the picture.

Date: _____

1 Look at the pictures. What does each device need to work?

Write **E** in the box if the device needs mains electricity to work.
Write **B** in the box if it needs batteries to work.

2 Look at the picture.

a Circle all the devices that need mains electricity to work.

b Colour in the devices that need batteries to work.

c Which device needs a battery and mains electricity to work?

_____

Now look at and think
about each of the
I can statements.

Date: _____

1 Draw lines from the magnet to the objects that are magnetic.

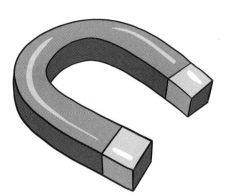

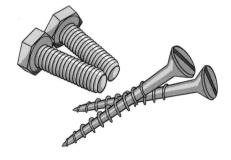

2 Look at Jakob's worksheet. Circle the mistakes Jakob has made.

Magnetic	Non-magnetic
padlock and key	rubber boot
metal spoon	wooden table
marbles	bicycle
scissors	shirt
eraser	iron nails
paperclips	book
bone	plant

Now look at and think about each of the *I can* statements.

Date: _____

1 Some things were done differently before electricity. Draw lines to match the old way of doing things to the new way.

| **Without electricity** | **With electricity** |

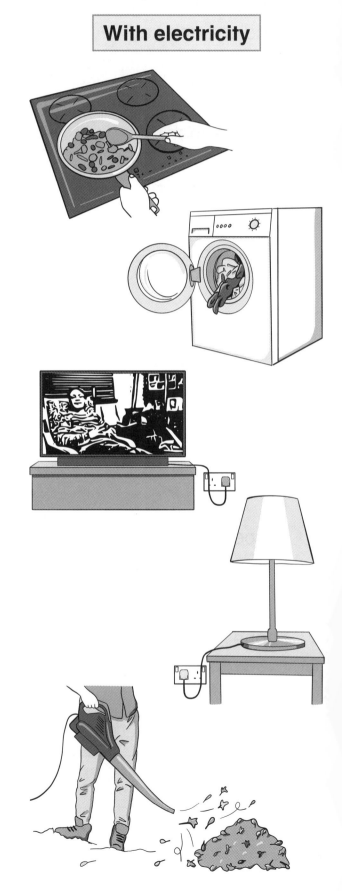

2 Look at the two sets of pictures. Describe how things have changed.

a

_____

_____

_____

_____

b

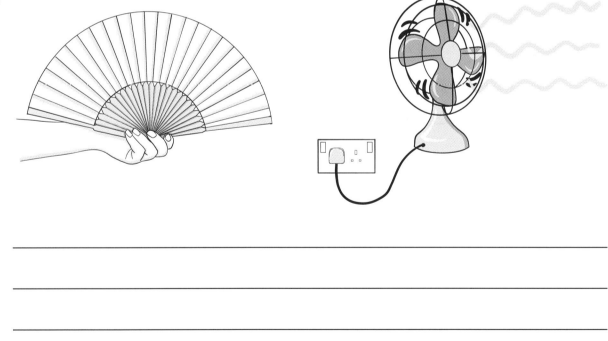

_____

_____

_____

_____

Now look at and think about each of the *I can* statements.

Date: _____

1   Class 1B are testing water from different sources. Look at the beakers of water.

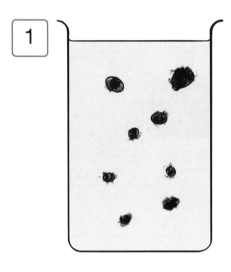

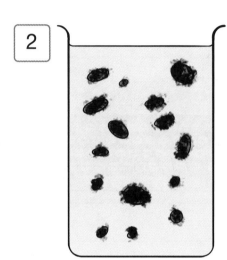

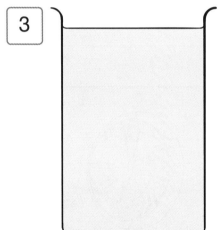

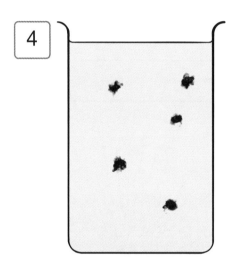

a Which beaker do you think has the cleanest water?

_____

b Which beaker do you think has the dirtiest water?

_____

2   Beaker 2 contains tap water.

a Do you think the children should drink water from the tap?

 Yes   No

b What should they do?

_____

3 Look at the picture. Class 1C are investigating a water filter.

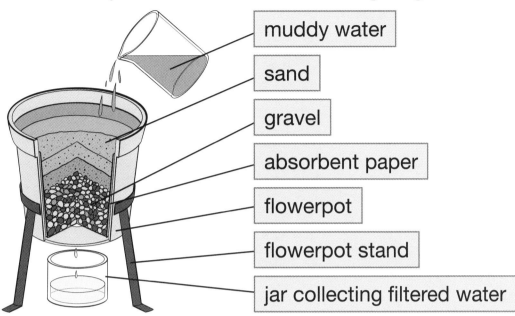

muddy water

sand

gravel

absorbent paper

flowerpot

flowerpot stand

jar collecting filtered water

a What equipment do the children need?

_____

_____

b Write the steps the children should follow to do this investigation.

_____

_____

_____

_____

_____

_____

c Predict the result of the investigation.

_____

Now look at and think about each of the *I can* statements.

Date: _____

Topic 6 Earth and Space

1 What is the name of the planet where we live?

_____

2 Add labels to the two different parts of planet Earth.

land   water

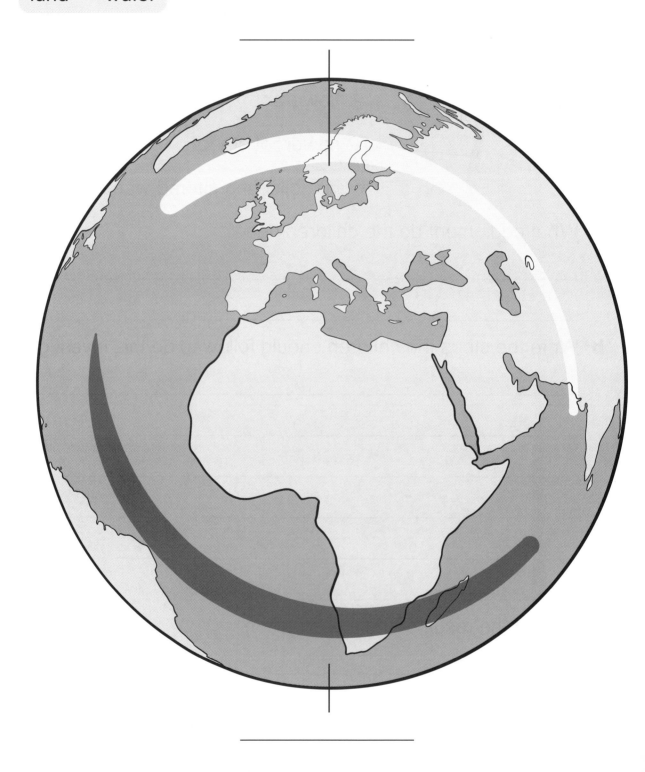

3 Name the different land and water features.

lake river forest mountains sea desert

Land	Water
_____	_____
_____	_____
_____	_____

4 Complete the sentences.

A _____ is land with very little water.

A _____ is land with lots of trees.

The _____ is water that is very salty.

A _____ is water that is not salty.

Now look at and think about each of the *I can* statements.

Date: _____

1 Describe what you can see in each picture.

a

_____

_____

_____

b

_____

_____

_____

2 How is water being wasted in these pictures?

3 Draw a picture to show how the water can be saved.

Wasting water	How is the water wasted?	How can the water be saved?
	_____ _____ _____	
	_____ _____ _____	
	_____ _____ _____	
	_____ _____ _____	
	_____ _____ _____	

Now look at and think about each of the *I can* statements.

Date: _____

1 Look at the pictures. What type of material is covering the land?

rocks   soil   pebbles   sand

_____   _____

_____   _____

2 What type of land do plants grow well in? _____

3 Label the different things you can see in the mound of soil.

earthworm   stick   leaf   stone
roots   woodlouse   ant

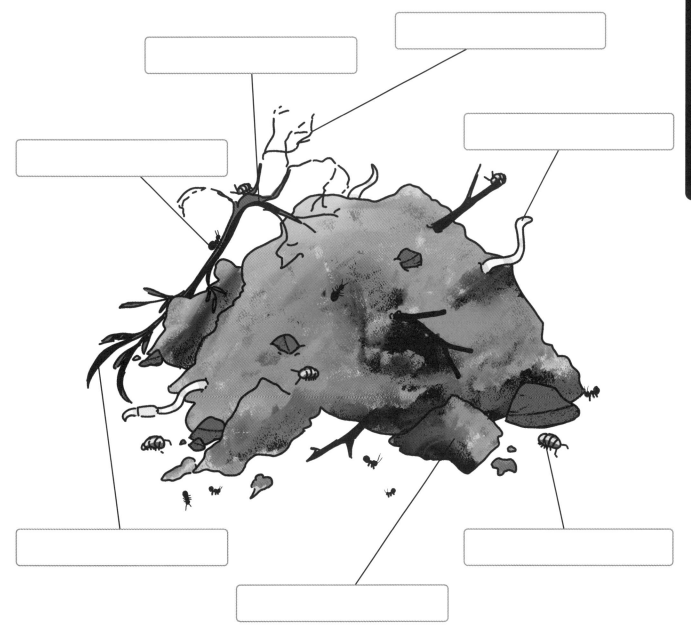

Now look at and think about each of the *I can* statements.

Date: _____

1 Circle the pictures of things that give us light.

2 Complete the sentences about the Sun
Use the words in the box to help you.

| alive | warm | night | star | light | day |

The Sun is a big _____.

The Sun gives the Earth _____ during the day.

The Sun keeps us _____ during the day.

We can see the Sun during the _____.

We cannot see the sun shining at _____.

The Sun is important to keep plants, humans and other

animals _____!

Now look at and think
about each of the
I can statements.

Date: _____

Summative assessment 3 (sidebar)

1 Look at the picture.

a Circle the things that use mains electricity.

b What things need batteries to work?

_____

2 Look at each picture. Is the object magnetic? Tick (✓) the correct answer.

Yes ☐ No ☐	Yes ☐ No ☐
Yes ☐ No ☐	Yes ☐ No ☐
Yes ☐ No ☐	Yes ☐ No ☐
Yes ☐ No ☐	Yes ☐ No ☐
Yes ☐ No ☐	Yes ☐ No ☐

3 Look at the pictures.

_____   _____

a Label the pictures **day** or **night**.

b How are the pictures different?

_____

_____

4 What does the Sun give us during the day?

_____

5 What would life be like without the Sun?

_____

6 Look at the picture. Write the labels. Use the words in the box.

mountain   forest   lake   river   soil   rock   pebbles

Date: _____